The Little Book of
BIG SQUARE
Mandalas 3

ISBN: 9781723716133

Join the conversation on facebook:

www.facebook.com/tabbystangledart

If you enjoyed this book, please consider taking a few minutes to leave a review on Amazon.

Please post your colored images online with **#tabbystangledart** or **#tabbyb** so I can find them easily.

Instagram: @tabbystangledart
Twitter: @tabbyleann
www.patreon.com/tabbyb
www.sellfy.com/tabbyb
www.redbubble.com/people/tabbyb
www.amazon.com/author/tabbystangledart
http://tinyurl.com/tabbytube

10217287R00055

Made in the USA
Lexington, KY
19 September 2018